GW01606249

LUTRA

The Story of an Otter

COLLINS ANIMAL LIVES

Other books in the series

TALPA The Story of a Mole
KENNETH MELLANBY

VULPINA The Story of a Fox
DAVID MACDONALD

CAPREOLUS The Story of a Roe Deer
RAYMOND E. CHAPLIN

SCIURUS The Story of a Grey Squirrel
JAN TAYLOR

LUTRA

The Story of an Otter

PHILIP WAYRE

Illustrated by John Edwards

COLLINS

For Lucy and Kate

William Collins Sons & Co Ltd
London · Glasgow · Sydney · Auckland
Toronto · Johannesburg

First published 1979

ISBN 0 00 195611 9
Made and Printed in Great Britain
by W & J Mackay & Co Ltd, Chatham, Kent

Contents

W
S
N
E
FEN
FEN
Holt
Holt
Heronry Wood
Sand Pit
Deserted Village
Village
Decoy Wood
Pipe
Mill
Solitary Farmhouse
Course of Old Railway
New Cut
Disused Pits
Lagoon
Coast Road
NATURE RESERVE
Old Bridge Holt
Thorn Bush Holt
Main Dyke
MARSH
SALTMARSH
Sluice Gate
Embankment Path
SAND
SALTINGS
MUD
Shingle Bar
NORTH SEA

Foreword

The otter is an uncommon, highly secretive and nocturnal animal, which does not tolerate any form of disturbance. This is why, so far as I know, none of the several books written in the past about the life of the otter has been based on scientific observation. In addition, its habit of wandering over a territory which may include more than fifteen kilometres of river makes regular observation even more difficult.

Lutra is an imaginary otter, but in telling her story I have tried to base her behaviour on scientific fact. To do this I have relied not only on my own observations, but on those of scientists like Vincent Weir, Jim Green, Sam Erlinge and Paul Chanin, all men who have made a special study of the otter.

So far as my own experiences go, I have been lucky in owning a number of tame otters of which four – Ripple, Lucy, Kate and Fury – have played leading roles. Their stories are told in one of my previous books, *The River People*. All were so tame that I was able to let them wander freely in the rivers and marshes of Norfolk as well as on the saltings along the coast.

Wherever they went I followed, sometimes on land, often in the water and sometimes below the surface. Wearing a wetsuit and aqualung I followed them into the depths of the mill pools and the clear reaches of the river, watching them turn over the stones in search of crayfish or rooting in the mud for eels. In this way I shared the otters' underwater world.

When Ripple's cubs were born I was able to film life inside an otter's holt. In time, both Kate and Fury bred, giving me further opportunities for observation.

The story of Lutra has been built up from all this material, while the descriptions of her home territory have been drawn from typical Norfolk rivers like the Waveney, Wensum and Stiffkey.

The otter in this story is called Lutra because that means "otter" in Latin.

I

Introducing Lutra

The river flowed gently, meandering through lush green water meadows, its course marked by scattered alders and a fringe of tall reeds. It was May and the sun, already low in the western sky, sent shafts of light stabbing into the clear depths.

As a rule Lutra would still have been asleep, curled up in the dry, hidden in a thicket of bramble or secure in a hole in the river bank. But on this particular evening she was out earlier than usual. For several days she had felt restless, a feeling which made her start her night's wanderings earlier and caused her to travel farther. Two and a half years old she was ready to breed for the first time.

Lutra was just over one metre long and

weighed six kilograms. Sometimes she swam slowly on the surface of the water, dog-paddling with all four webbed feet, her body just awash so that her flattish head carved a V-shaped wake. This way she could watch the swallows diving from the sky to skim the water in their search for insects and see the great black and white cows that munched the sweet spring grass so noisily. Carried by the current she played beneath the alder trees which lined the river bank, their boughs heavy with golden catkins. A song thrush sang to his mate from the very top of one of the trees – "See you, see you, you all right? You all right?"

In May the water was still cold, but Lutra was insulated by her fur which never became water-logged. The dense velvet-like layer next to her skin was protected by an outer covering of much longer guard hairs. A cushion of air trapped between these two layers of hair prevented the water from penetrating.

When she wanted to travel more quickly Lutra took a deep breath and dived beneath the surface. Then she swam swiftly, driving herself through the water by powerful up and down strokes of her hind quarters and tail. She kept her front paws tucked in close to her sides to streamline her body, but kicked powerfully

with her larger webbed hind feet. Then she travelled faster than a man could walk, but since she could hold her breath for only a minute or two she had to surface regularly to breathe.

Every time she dived, a string of bubbles rose to the surface as the water pressure forced some of the air out of her coat.

When running on land, which she did with an awkward-looking lope, her back arched, Lutra relied chiefly on her hearing to keep her out of danger. Although her ears were small they were extremely sensitive. Her sense of smell was also good, but by comparison her sight was poor, although she could see remarkably well underwater in clear conditions.

The sun flickered and dappled the pale green beds of water-lilies, the crinkled cabbage-like submerged leaves often browned by a fine layer of silt deposited by the lazy current. Lutra looked down at the shoals of tiny fish, minnows, roachlings and rudd which hung in clouds, suspended in the clear water. They darted this way and that, flashing silver sparklets as they suddenly turned, but they were too small for Lutra to bother to chase them.

Rounding a bend she found herself in shallow water where the river ran over a firm bottom covered by a dense growth of grass-green pondweed. Looking down she saw the sinister shape of a pike lying motionless, striped russet and black in the sunlight. Its body was half hidden in the weed as it lay in wait for its prey, a tiger of the underwater world.

When the evening light began to fade Lutra came to a deep stretch. Dull grey shapes moved far below her, and when they crossed a patch of pale sand she saw they were fat roach. One of them was blemished by two white spots of fungus on its broad back, the result of an earlier injury. Waggling their tails from side to side the shoal disappeared down a pathway between the ribbon-like leaves of arrowhead which trailed upwards towards the light.

Lutra dived and followed them through the forest of weed, the silence broken only by the thrumming of the water in her ears. Although she could no longer see the fish she knew exactly where they were from the vibrations in the water picked up by her stiff sensitive whiskers which acted as a kind of radar.

The roach with the fungus spots turned in an effort to escape, but Lutra swept up from beneath. She seized it in her front paws and continued up to the surface with the fish in her mouth. She came ashore on a low-lying spit of land and, after listening for sounds of danger, settled down at the water's edge and ate the roach, holding it in her front paws and crunching noisily. By the time she had finished only a patch of silver scales and a few small bones remained.

The fish had weighed nearly 200 grams and, although Lutra would need at least one more meal of similar size during the night, for the moment she was no longer hungry.

Running up the bank she rolled in the grass drying her chest and chin by rubbing herself on the ground from side to side with snake-like movements. Then she rolled over with her feet in the air, squirming this way and that to dry her back.

A healthy otter's coat starts to shed water as soon as the animal comes to land. First it breaks into a pattern of spikelets, then after the otter has shaken itself and rolled on the ground its fur is dry, although the outer surface remains damp.

After drying herself Lutra ran out on to the spit of land where the river turned sharply. She paused and smelled the ground carefully. Then she scratched up a tuft of grass, turned round, and with her tail raised, deposited her faeces, called spraint, on top of it. Otters regularly use the same places in which to leave their spraint. This is one of the ways in which each individual otter marks out its territory or home ground. Lutra had often used the tip of the spit, but tonight there was a lingering smell in the grass which excited her and she knew the dog otter had passed that way a few nights earlier.

A couple of kilometres downstream Lutra came to the road bridge. She could see the lights of the village beyond the poplar plantation and hear the noise of human voices. A dog barked and after a while a man shouted and a door banged.

All otters are curious by nature and the bridge held a certain fascination for Lutra. That night as she slipped downstream towards it she heard the sound of whispered voices, then she caught sight of two figures silhouetted against the sky. A car, its headlights piercing the darkness, came round the bend and the couple on the bridge moved on, caught for a moment in the dazzling beams.

Lutra dived, surfacing in the black vault

beneath the bridge. In the hollow silence water dripped from the damp arch above her. This was the dark and secretive world that only otters know. Here the river's edge was muddy, but against the stone column supporting the bridge it was drier. Lutra left the water, for this was a regular sprainting place. Once again her pulse quickened and she knew the dog otter had travelled that way.

In the morning the man saw Lutra's rounded footprints in the mud beneath the bridge and knew she had been there.

2
Decoy Wood

As dawn approached a pale grey light grew in the eastern sky. Lutra had been travelling downstream for three nights, and now she was almost at the limit of her home ground which included nearly ten kilometres of river from the fen near its headwaters down to the wide expanse of flat grazing marshes at the start of the estuary.

She had caught and eaten two more small fish during the night, another roach and a silvery bream. Now she was looking for a safe place in which to lie up and sleep during the day.

A grey mist hung like a curtain across the marshes as the sun rose, a silver ball low in the sky. A sedge warbler rasped its spring song from a thicket of bramble close to the water's edge and unseen lapwings wailed their cries of courtship from the far distance.

The sound of trickling water had drawn Lutra like a magnet. It came from a land drain put in by a farmer to take the water from a spring rising in a nearby meadow. The end of the pipe projected a short distance from the steep bank on the edge of a bend in the river where the current had carved away some of the peaty earth. Lutra lay on her back, letting the cold water splash on her chest and belly while she tried to catch the silver cascade in her front paws. It was fun and she rolled and spun in the river beneath the pipe. Sometimes she opened her mouth and spluttered and gulped as she tried to swallow the trickle, only to shake her head violently when she nearly choked.

Tiring of the game Lutra swam on downstream. She was making for the reed-fringed dyke which led away from the river across the marsh and ended in a swampy wood where, a hundred years before, men had built a duck decoy to trap the wildfowl which arrived every autumn from their breeding grounds in the far north of Europe and Russia.

The decoy had not been used for thirty years, but some of the wooden hoops of the trap still remained half buried in a jungle of nettles,

thistles and bramble. The old decoy pond, hidden among the trees where once tame ducks attracted their wild cousins, was choked with reeds, sedge and clumps of alder growing knee-deep in the stagnant water. Some of the larger trees had fallen in winter gales; only their trunks remained, rotting and moss-covered.

To reach Decoy Wood Lutra swam down the middle of the dyke. On each side of her the brown stalks of last year's thistles were clear cut against the sky. A tangled mass of cress, water plantain and water forget-me-not grew along the edges of the dyke. In places the weeds stretched right across the channel and Lutra had to push her way through.

Gradually the mist melted away in the sun's warmth; larks began to sing as they climbed high over the marsh. This was a flat, empty landscape and, apart from Decoy Wood, almost treeless. Instead the distant horizon was marked by windmills used for pumping the water from the low-lying ditches and dykes up into the river which flowed between banks raised above the grazing lands. Some of the mills were derelict, their place taken by modern electric or diesel pumps.

A single oak gatepost, leaning at an angle and black with age, was all that remained of a gateway between two marshes where long ago men had built a bridge of wooden railway sleepers across the dyke. The bridge was still sound though slippery with algae which grew on the damp surface.

As Lutra swam towards the wood she heard a noise drawing nearer as the water in the dyke began to shiver. Instinctively she dived and hid in the gloom beneath the bridge. The sound grew into a roar and Lutra dived again, her heart pounding with fear.

When she surfaced the noise was already dying away as the three horses galloped off snorting in the cold morning air, their manes and tails streaming in the wind.

As the otter slipped quietly into Decoy Wood a wren began to scold and woodpigeons flew off with a clatter of wings. Lutra left the water to spraint on a tussock of grass grown extra green from previous use. Half swimming, half sludging through the soft black mud she made her way to a large alder tree lying on what had once been an island in the centre of the pond. Honey-suckle trailed from its moss covered roots and a tangle of bramble guarded its hollow trunk accessible only through a hole in the underside.

Lutra rolled in the dead leaves on the island, shook herself and then slipping beneath the brambles crawled up through the hole and curled up to sleep on the soft wood inside the rotting trunk, just as her mother had done a week before Lutra had been born.

3
Lutra Finds a Mate

Safe and dry inside the hollow trunk Lutra slept soundly, not waking until noon when the noise of a tractor working at the far side of the marsh disturbed her.

During the afternoon she slept fitfully, often lying awake listening to the skylarks and a great tit greeting the spring with his metallic song. His mate was already sitting on a clutch of nine tiny eggs, whitish in colour speckled with reddish-brown. Her snug nest of moss and cow's hair plucked from the marsh's many barbed-wire fences was concealed deep down inside a hollow willow-stump.

Only when the daylight had faded and a new moon rode crescent-shaped in the dark sky did Lutra leave Decoy Wood and return along the dyke to the river, pushing her way through clumps of water violet and crowfoot. Sometimes the pungent peppermint scent of water mint growing amongst the meadowsweet along the edge of the dyke overpowered the rank smell of the black mud.

Back in the main river Lutra again followed the current. Almost at once she was alarmed by a loud rustling on the bank followed by a splash. Instinctively she dived only to discover that whatever was there had also submerged and was swimming upstream.

Her curiosity aroused, Lutra turned to follow and being much faster she soon caught up with the harmless coypu. The lumbering rodent, almost as big as an otter, was a native of South America, but more than forty years ago men had brought it to England and farmed it for its fur called nutria. When the fashion in furs changed some of the animals had been set free and many of them had colonized the waterways of East Anglia where Lutra lived.

Unknown to Lutra her scent had been borne downstream by the current and carried by the westerly breeze. The dog otter had caught it and was already travelling upstream to meet her. He was much larger than Lutra, a fine animal in his sixth year and weighing nearly ten kilograms. His home range was more than twice the size of Lutra's and extended beyond the wide grazing marshes to the sea, across five kilometres of saltings and up another river valley towards the city.

Lutra first caught sight of the dog otter round a bend in the river when she saw a dark object swimming towards her low in the water, leaving a silvery suspicion of a wake rippling in the moonlight.

She lay motionless on the surface, carried by the current, alert and watchful, waiting. As the object drew closer she "huffed", an otter's way of saying "Who or what are you?"

The dog otter came straight on. Lutra huffed again and dived. When she surfaced the dog otter was close by. Lutra chittered, a high pitched querulous sound warning him to keep away, but he swam towards her whickering a low gentle greeting.

Gaining confidence Lutra remained on the surface, watching. The dog otter dived and came up in front of her. She slipped beneath the surface, turned on her back, completed the roll and swam away, but when she came up he was still there. Whatever she did the dog otter was always just behind her.

Lutra left the water and ran up the bank and out into the meadow, but the dog otter still followed her. Soon he caught up and whickered again. Lutra chittered back, but he took no notice. Instead he rolled her over nibbling playfully at her neck and behind her ears. Lutra tore herself free and ran away, but the dog otter soon caught her and rolled her over again.

This time Lutra lay still and the dog otter continued to nuzzle her. When he suddenly ran off Lutra jumped and followed him. They gambolled and chased one another, rolling and

wrestling now on land now back in the river.

Sometimes they dived, chasing each other far below in the darkness of the weed beds only to surface in mock battle, turning, twisting, spinning, sending showers of silver bubbles on to the moonlit surface of the river.

In the early hours of the morning when the moon had set and the sky closed in, black with cloud, the otters paused in their courtship. Hunger drove them to hunt and soon the dog otter swam to the bank, a large bream in his mouth. Lutra followed landing beside him, and when she sniffed at the fish he picked it up in his jaws and ran off into the meadow. She gave chase and he returned to the river dropping his quarry at the water's edge as he disappeared into the dark depths in search of another.

Lutra seized the bream and ran off with it to hide in a clump of sedge where she ate it in peace. She heard the dog otter surface several times, then there was silence followed by the unmistakable crunching sound as he broke into another fish on the far bank.

Later that night Lutra caught two roach and the dog a fat chub. In the morning the man noticed the tell-tale patches of scales on the river bank. As the sky paled towards dawn the otters left the river and crossed the marsh

towards the embankment which once carried the single track railway.

Beyond the embankment lay a series of flooded gravel workings, some of them covering several hectares. Their banks were often sheer, falling straight down to deeps where, even in daytime, little light penetrated and no plants grew on the grey slimy bottom. Fish were scarce in these barren depths for there was little food. When the otters dived and skimmed over the floor of the pit they found only a length of rusting steel hawser and an empty oil drum half buried in the mud.

The shallower areas where a man could nearly stand were different. Crisp green pondweed grew like a lawn; crowfoot and arrowhead trailed upwards to float on the surface in a tangle of broad leaves. Fish were numerous but

Lutra and the dog otter left them alone and made their way to the reed bed growing in the shallows. The place was rarely disturbed by people and the two otters curled up on a couch of flattened reed where a mound of gravel formed a small island.

Shortly before dusk the otters were awake and hungry. Lutra woke first. Yawning she stretched her body full length on the ground, reaching out as far as she could with her front paws. Then she rolled on her back, arched her neck upwards and nibbled the fur on her chest and belly. Rolling on her side she groomed her flanks in the same way before getting up and walking slowly to a small pile of stones at the end of the islet. After some seconds of careful sniffing she turned round and deposited her spraint on top of it. The dog otter, his grooming finished, followed her to spraint in the same place.

They left the gravel pits and went back across the marsh. Several times they disturbed roosting lapwings which flapped away with mournful cries and once a snipe rose zig-zagging into the dark sky with a harsh "scarp scarp".

When they reached the river, the waxing moon was high causing the stars to lose some of their brilliance. They swam and dived together, but there was something about Lutra that was different. When the dog otter chased her she seemed willing to be caught. When he closed with her biting her neck in play she no longer chittered at him and dived, but made only a half-hearted attempt to escape.

During one of their mock fights Lutra suddenly lay still, floating with her rudder slightly arched. The dog otter swam alongside, seized her round the loins with his front paws while his jaws locked on a fold of skin in the nape of her neck. Lutra made no effort to shake him off.

They remained coupled for more than twenty minutes, rolling spinning and diving as one animal. Sometimes they remained below for so long that Lutra gasped for breath when they eventually surfaced. Finally, their mating over, they separated.

Together they continued on downstream, fishing as they went. If the quarry was very small, and sticklebacks were plentiful in these reaches, the otters crunched them as they swam. When they caught larger fish, rudd and perch, they swam to the bank to eat them on the grass at the waterside.

During the night they passed through the New Cut, a long straight stretch of river between high banks bare of reeds or other vegetation. They came to the upper reaches of the estuary and Lutra noticed the salty taste of the water which was no longer sparkling and clear but thick with grey-brown sediment.

By dawn they were in a new world. Great reed beds lay on each side of the channel which became wider all the time. Seabirds called and gulls flew inland in arrowhead formation against the grey sky. Lutra could just hear the roar of the North Sea surf surging across distant sand-bars, a sound she had heard as a cub long ago when her mother had brought her here.

4
The Saltings

They spent the day sleeping, hidden on a couch of flattened reed not far from the edge of the channel.

Three hours after the sun had set behind a great bank of dark cloud, and the moon was already high, they began their night's fishing, following the river down towards the sea.

The dog otter still remained close to Lutra and they mated again before midnight, rolling and diving together as they drifted down towards the great sluice gate in the embankment which kept the winter sea at bay.

The coast road ran along the top of the bank and they watched the lights of passing cars. Finding the sluice gate closed against the incoming tide they left the river and waited,

hidden in the long grass at the foot of the slope, while a car went by. The dog otter was the first to cross the road. Lutra, suspicious of the unfamiliar surface, hesitated. Once she got half way across, only to dash back as the lights of another car appeared.

The dog otter kept calling her, a single high-pitched squeak which sounded like a thin piercing whistle repeated at short intervals. Finally Lutra dashed across to join him only to be caught in the full glare of the headlights of a car rounding the bend beyond the river.

Although Lutra did not know it, the great saltmarsh sprawled along the coast for many kilometres on both sides of her. Beyond it lay wide expanses of flat yellow sand and dark mud which ended where the seafoam hissed at the edge of the oncoming tide which crept slowly shorewards filling and finally submerging the wind runnels in the sand.

At half tide steep banks of glistening mud marked the channel. Small crabs were numerous and easy to catch in the murky water. The otters ate several, holding them in their front paws, crunching them as they swam.

Lutra caught quite a large one, nearly a hand's width across its shell, with big pincer claws which nipped her. Surfacing she played with it, spurred on by its mass of struggling spiky legs. The crab managed to get a hold on Lutra's upper lip with one of its claws and she had to shake her head violently to dislodge it. The crab immediately sidled away down towards the bed of the channel, but Lutra dived and caught it again. She kept letting it go to have the fun of recapturing it until, tired of the game, she lost interest and the crab reached the muddy bottom of the channel where it quickly buried itself.

The flood tide brought all sorts of fish up the river and the otters found small flounders, locally called flukes, a tasty change from a freshwater diet.

Unlike the silence of the inland grazing marshes the night was full of noises heard against the dull boom of distant breakers. Terns, lately arrived from Africa where they had spent the winter, kept up a chorus of harsh cries from the shingle spit at the edge of the

salting where a few pairs had already laid their mottled eggs in shallow scrapes on the shore.

Oystercatchers, resplendent in their black and white uniform, tripped lightly at the tide's edge trilling their spring song through half open, carmine red bills.

In the pale light before dawn Lutra and the dog otter were swimming along the edge of the salting. The tide still had an hour to flow. The sand-bars had disappeared and the rising water had already filled the creeks and runnels which patterned the marsh. Gradually the sea took over, drowning the green expanse so that the tallest spikes of sea lavender and sea purslane were all that remained above the silver-grey surface.

The dog otter led Lutra out towards the breakers, a small swell lifting them rhythmically. The first line of surf broke and came

sweeping in. Both otters dived, surfacing in the quiet water beyond, only to turn and chase the receding wave. Growing bolder they swam farther out to roll and play in the breakers. It was exhilarating and they were so busy that they ignored a whelk boat passing seaward down the main estuary, although they heard the throb of its diesel engine.

When the tide began to ebb it carried the otters in a northerly direction past the nesting terns which came to meet them in a screaming horde, diving at them in mock attack. Farther down the coast the dog otter led Lutra ashore on a high ridge of shingle where a pair of oystercatchers, whose nest was nearby, immediately mobbed them. Like the terns the birds relied on camouflage to protect their large pebble-blotched eggs lying in a scrape among the stones.

The sea never quite covered the shingle bank except in winter when north-westerly gales coincided with a period of extra high tides driving the breakers right across the marsh to beat against the foot of the seawall. Nothing remained of the salting then, only the gulls tossed like pieces of paper in the wind as they battled with the storm above the sea.

Running along the top of the ridge, the otters explored the line of flotsam left by the last high tide of winter when the waves had torn loose vast quantities of seaweed and rolled it up the beach. Along with the weed had come a great variety of objects, driftwood, some of it black with age, the empty purselike cases of dog-fish eggs and those of whelk like tight bunches of grapes of which only the parchment-dry skin remained.

A dead seal lay buried in the weed; the otters picked up the scent of the rotting carcass long before they came to it. A neat hole in its flank showed where the bullet fired from a fishing boat had ended its life.

Lutra found the wind-dried remains of a gull, a few discoloured feathers still clinging to the bones. She carried it a little way before dropping it. There was an unnatural smell about it which came also from the dark patches on the beach.

The first few drops of rain fell soon after dawn and the dog otter led the way across the salting towards the land. Often they disturbed redshanks feeding in the emptying creeks, and the birds would jump up with hysterical calls of alarm "clee clee clee tui tui".

When they reached a wide creek the otters slid down the slippery bank into the mud-brown water, Lutra following the dog as he swam. He was making for the seawall and the fresh marsh beyond it where he knew of a safe place to lie up for the day.

Clumps of gorse grew at the foot of the high embankment where a track ran along the edge of the salting. The otters half-heartedly chased a rabbit which soon disappeared down a hole. Then they ran up the grassy slope and down the other side into the fresh marsh, plunging into a reed-filled dyke to lap the brackish water as they swam, for they were thirsty after their night's hunting in the saltmarsh.

They lay up that day in a dense thicket of nettles and bramble in a corner of the marsh. Lutra woke several times to nibble and bite the fur on her left forefoot. The black oil she had picked up on the shore tasted rancid and soon her foot was inflamed and sore. Once she slipped into the dyke to drink and the cold water soothed the irritation.

That night the dog otter returned to the salting but Lutra stayed behind in the fresh marsh. Her foot hurt when she ran on land and there were frogs and eels in the ditches which were easy to catch.

The foot took a full three weeks to heal and at first Lutra shunned the sea marshes where the salt water stung her inflamed pad. By night she hunted the ditches and reedy pools of the fresh marshes varying her diet of sticklebacks and eels with the occasional young mallard. Well grown but not yet able to fly, the ducklings were easy to catch as they flapped across the water or hid at the edge of the reeds.

Sometimes the dog otter hunted with Lutra, but more often he returned to the saltings to range far and wide over his territory. Often he covered as much as ten kilometres in a single night, and once dawn found him back in Decoy Wood more than fifteen kilometres distant.

When not fishing he travelled much of the time on land. Where the riverside vegetation had been cleared the naked banks afforded no cover should danger threaten. Then he took to the meadows, taking short cuts between bends in the river, loping along at nearly ten kilometres an hour. In this way he covered the barren unfriendly stretches in a surprisingly short time.

By midsummer day Lutra was back in the estuary moving upstream to more familiar territory. By day she lay up in the reeds or made a temporary couch hidden among the luxuriant growth of meadowsweet, ragged robin and willowherb which covered the banks.

Often she saw the dog otter, and sometimes they fished together or played "catch me if you can", chasing one another, diving, porpoising, rolling and lunging at each other until the surface of the river boiled. Sometimes they rushed up the bank and out into the meadow; then Lutra would suddenly drop flat, belly pressed to the ground, as she hid behind a clump of thistles waiting her chance to leap out at the dog otter as he came by.

As the days passed Lutra felt a new urge; she became less playful and more intent on her journey upstream. She was making for Heronry Wood three kilometres beyond the farm where the pink house stood alone overlooking the wide expanse of the river valley. It was over a month since the otters had mated and Lutra, perhaps without knowing why, wanted to be far away, alone and safe in a dry holt where no man ever came.

5
Search for a Holt

Below Heronry Wood the river narrowed, wandering through rough meadows studded with ancient thorn bushes. The wood itself lay beyond what remained of an old osier carr where many years ago willows were carefully grown and pruned to provide supple branches for making baskets, creels and eel traps.

Alder trees had long since invaded the carr together with clumps of tussock sedge and bull rush. A reed-filled dyke ran through the centre linking Herony Wood with the river.

In this overgrown swamp the soft mud was so deep in places that a man could easily drown, trapped in the stinking black ooze. Lutra passed through in the inky darkness just after midnight when the marsh was silent, save for the distant whine of a motor bike on the main road and the ghostlike croaks and snores of fledgling herons fidgeting in their massive nests high in the alder trees.

Lack of sunlight prevented the growth of reeds beneath the trees so that the black water of the dyke was clear, the bottom covered with last year's fallen leaves. A large ash tree stood on the left bank with twin roots, as thick as a man's thighs, sloping down into the water. Between them the constant damp had rotted the base of the trunk forming a dark cavern. Lutra swam inside and found she could easily dig her way through the soft wood at the back of the recess and into the bank behind it.

Before dawn she had tunnelled into the bank and had hollowed out a nest-chamber well above water level. The effort had made her hungry, and at first light she returned to the osier carr where she soon caught an unsuspecting moorhen.

At sun-up the noise in the wood rose to a climax of squawks and yelps interspersed with staccato bill-snapping as the heronry awoke and the hungry youngsters clambered about the topmost branches calling for food.

Many of the adult herons had left the wood before dawn and were now returning, their crops bulging with eels and frogs for their

querulous young. As each bird alighted clumsily in the trees its offspring climbed towards it, its clamour for food rising to a crescendo and dying away in sobbing gulps as the parent opened its beak and regurgitated the semi-digested mess into its young bird's maw.

Beneath the trees the ground was splashed white with droppings and the sun-dried pellets of indigestible fish scales and bone cast by the birds. In Heronry Wood the air was foetid, heavy and dank.

During the following night Lutra made several journeys from her holt beneath the ash tree to the dyke in order to gather reed and sedge with which she lined her den. Tearing mouthfuls of vegetation where it grew thickest at the side of the dyke she swam back, holding it in her jaws. Sometimes she picked up twigs the thickness of a pencil from the floor of the wood and carried them into her nest.

When Lutra had finished, the hollow was almost full of damp vegetation. Turning round and round she pulled it into shape so that finally she lay snug inside a hollow ball of reed, sedge, grass and twigs which completely covered her. The twigs might seem uncomfortable but they served a special function in preventing the nest becoming a soggy mat by allowing air to circulate through it and the damp from Lutra's coat to disperse quickly.

Lutra added to the nest on successive nights bringing in more material on her way back from the river when she had been out hunting for fish.

By day she lay snug in her holt dozing or lying awake listening to the noise of the heronry and the monotonous chirring song of a reed warbler. The slender, soberly-coloured little birds had built their tiny nest over the water of the dyke by weaving feathery reed tops and fine grasses into a deep cup cleverly attached to three swaying reed stems. It was so deep that when the hen sat on her four mottled eggs she disappeared completely below the rim. Even in a strong wind, when the whole reed bed bowed crazily this way and that, there was no risk of the eggs falling out.

Early one morning Lutra, asleep in her holt, was suddenly awakened by the noise of shouting, sticks banging on tree trunks and the barking of dogs. A vixen had been raiding the rearing field on a nearby estate, taking the young pheasants to feed her cubs and now the gamekeepers were out in force to track her down and shoot her. Every piece of rough ground, every spinney and alder carr was to be scoured for the marauder, and Heronry Wood was high on their list.

The plan was simple. On reaching a wood three men with guns walked quietly round to the far side, deploying themselves to cover every likely escape route. The rest then lined out with their dogs and guns and beat through the wood making a great commotion to rouse any fox that might be lying up.

Lutra, alarmed by the noise and the dogs, instinctively left the safety of her holt, slipped into the dyke and made for the osier carr.

6

Birth of the Cubs

The three men had reached the far side of Heronry Wood and one of them wearing rubber boots had picked his way over the quaking turf between the wood and the osier carr to stand hidden behind the trunk of a fallen tree. He was thirty paces from the dyke and had a good view along the edge of the wood in each direction. Other men stood at each corner, hidden by the trees.

Lutra lay submerged except for the top of her head, completely hidden by a curtain of tussock sedge at the side of the dyke. A jay flew overhead shrieking harshly and two moorhens skittered down the drain.

As the noise drew closer Lutra slid beneath the surface and swam away. She came up to breathe and the din was louder than ever. She dived again.

The man was watching a brood of young mallard skulking through the reeds when he noticed a string of bubbles. Seconds later Lutra surfaced, but dived again before he could raise his gun.

The man ran a few steps towards the dyke and waited. He knew the otter had to come up for air again soon and its pelt was worth at least ten pounds from the dealer in Wisbech.

When Lutra next broke surface she was hidden by reeds, but as she swam they moved and the man saw the sign. Raising his gun he took careful aim ahead of the moving reed stems and squeezed the trigger. As he did so the morning sun glinted on his gun barrels and Lutra, twenty paces away, saw it and dived at once.

The pattern of shot ripped into the water as her rudder slid below the surface. Lutra swam as she had never swum before, driving herself through the reeds with all the strength in her back and hind legs. When next she was forced to come up for air she was on the river side of the osier carr and moments later she left the dyke for the river itself and turned downstream.

She kept close to the bank, exploring every

hole and overhang cut by the current. Whenever possible she surfaced beneath trailing vegetation so that for the most part she went unseen. On the way she caught several small roach and ate them lying up beneath the bank, anchoring herself to the muddy wall with one hind foot, only her head above water.

Below the solitary farmhouse, Lutra found a coypu run leading from the water's edge up the bank and into a jungle of sedge and bramble. The place was littered with the discarded mother-of-pearl shells of swan mussels which the otherwise vegetarian rodents had opened and eaten. Rats too had joined in the feast, diving for the molluscs wherever the water was shallow, for only the coypu could reach the bottom in the deeper stretches. Lutra ignored the mussels. Her teeth were designed for cutting flesh and crunching bone and were useless when it came to chiselling through thick shell. Making her way into the centre of the thicket she found a place where the coypu had formed a rough nest of rushes bitten neatly through as though cut by scissors. In it she curled up and slept.

The sun was already sending long shadows across the marsh when Lutra awoke, stretched and yawned before returning to the top of the bank where she paused to spraint. An early

barn owl was floating across the meadows, a white spectre on thistle-down wings silently following the twisting course of the river, watching the banks below for an unsuspecting water vole.

Soon after midnight Lutra passed through the barren waters of the New Cut and out into the upper reaches of the yellow-brown estuary. Sometimes she disturbed roosting gulls which rose without a sound and vanished into the darkness.

On reaching the edge of the saltings she left the river and ran up the grass slope of the seawall and down the other side, before slipping into the main dyke which drained the fresh marshes.

Dawn came, white and heavy with mist, so that Lutra could see nothing beyond the reeds growing on both banks. Somewhere on the marsh cows coughed in the damp air, and from far out to sea the foghorn on a light vessel moaned and grunted. A party of bearded reedlings passed, flitting from reed stem to swaying reed stem, the family of two adults and six youngsters calling to each other with a musical "ping ping" to keep contact.

The marshes ran parallel with the shore, their reed beds and pools of brackish water giving way to shingle at the foot of the great bank, their only defence against winter storms. Lutra could hear the regular thud and surge of the sea, sullen and grey in the fog. Less than a kilometre inland, and almost in the centre of the eight-kilometre stretch of marshland lay the biggest reed bed, and right in the middle of it a clump of thorn bushes broke up the otherwise regular skyline of waving reeds.

The bushes grew on a low hummock of dry land surrounded by water, and beneath them a tangle of bramble, nettles and cleavers fought for the sunlight. The thorns were very old and one of them, torn down in a winter gale, lay on its side, lodged against its neighbour. Brambles covered its roots, and beneath the main trunk the ground was firm and dry.

Lutra felt secure here, and after scratching a shallow depression in the soil she curled up and slept through the long hours of daylight. When night came she returned to the main dyke and caught an easy meal of eels, nosing them out of the thick mud with uncanny accuracy. After she had eaten several she happened to catch a large one more than seventy-five centimetres long. Twice it managed to struggle free, but each time Lutra swam in pursuit and seized it again. Finally she surfaced with the eel firmly clamped in her jaws.

In no hurry to eat, Lutra carried her quarry away from the dyke and out on to the grass. There she dropped it while she rolled, rubbing her chin and face from side to side to rid herself of the eel's slime. She appeared to ignore her victim as it began to writhe snake-like through the grass in the direction of the dyke; but just when it seemed to have escaped she ran after it, and seizing it by the tail tossed it cart-wheeling into the air. As it fell she pounced on it, throwing it up again and again, rushing this way and that, sometimes catching it in her mouth only to toss it wildly from side to side. When she tired of the game she lay down, holding the eel between her front paws while she noisily crunched its head. It took her nearly half an hour to finish her meal.

Later that night Lutra, exploring the reed bed, suddenly stopped and listened intently. From the direction of the dyke she had heard the high-pitched whistle of an otter. It was repeated, closer this time and Lutra ran to meet the stranger. At the edge of the dyke she stopped and called. Immediately there came an answering whistle as the dog otter swam towards her. Lutra recognized him as he left the water and she caught his scent.

Whickering in greeting the dog sniffed her face, then rolled her over in fun, but Lutra was in no mood for play. Getting up she plunged into the dyke, and when he tried to continue the game she turned on him chittering angrily. That day both otters slept beneath the thorn bushes but in the evening the dog otter left to patrol another part of his territory beyond the estuary.

Lutra made her second holt below the roots of the fallen thorn digging out a shallow burrow hidden by tangled vegetation. Again she made repeated journeys to gather reed, sedge and tufts of grass to line the chamber.

One night early in July Lutra remained in the holt. It was nine weeks since she and the dog otter had mated and an inner sense told her that something was about to happen. In the early hours before dawn her first cub was born to be followed after a few minutes by a second. Lutra was puzzled and the first tiny bird-like twitter, so small it might have come from a mouse, startled her. But when the cubs started to squirm, lying on their backs feebly moving their tiny legs she began to lick them tenderly between her front paws.

Soon they were dry and presently they began to twitter, nosing about in the warm fur of Lutra's belly in search of her teats and the life-giving milk. Lutra kept the cubs hidden, curling her body tightly round them so that they lay snugly enveloped by her fur.

7
Thorn Bush Holt

The cubs were no bigger than small rats, their little bodies covered with silvery-grey velvet and their heads were disproportionately large while their squat noses were so pink they might have been raw. Their eyes were tightly closed, and their salmon-pink paws were all they were able to move — apart from their tiny rudders which wagged in ecstasy when at last their feeble nuzzling found a teat.

While they drank they pushed each front pad rhythmically against their mother's belly to stimulate the flow of milk. When full they lay quite still, hidden in the warm circle of her body. Every two hours or so they woke and began to twitter with hunger as they searched for their next meal.

Life inside Thorn Bush holt was dark and secretive and for the most part silent. Lutra spent much of the time dozing, waking at intervals to nibble and groom her cubs. If one of them attempted to crawl out from beneath her she seized it by the scruff of the neck, and after every feed she held each in turn on its back between her front paws while she licked its anal area. This stimulated the cub to relieve itself with much tail wagging. Lutra licked up the droppings, keeping the holt spotlessly clean.

It was almost twenty four hours before she left the cubs, and then she was gone only long enough to drink at the edge of the reed bed. On their own for the first time, the cubs squirmed and twittered in the darkness.

Each bout of suckling lasted about ten minutes, and as the cubs grew stronger they fed less frequently, often going three or four hours between meals. Lutra could turn round in a complete circle, still keeping her cubs hidden. Usually she slept resting her head on her back or rudder, her eyes almost closed but still showing white through tiny slits.

On the second evening after their birth, Lutra left the cubs for nearly an hour. She was hungry and it was still daylight when she reached the main dyke. Reed warblers were rasping their song in the heavy evening air, clouds of sedge flies rose and fell in their courtship dance over the still water while bats swept past on urgent wings, hawking flies. Lutra listened to the click and squeak of their echo-location system which guided them unerringly on to their targets.

Eels, partially nocturnal, were active in the warm water of the drain creeping sinuously across the dark mud snatching anything they could find from worms to small fish and smaller eels. Once caught, little escaped their rows of sharp teeth.

Lutra ate four eels and rolled in the grass to dry her coat before returning to her cubs. As soon as she entered the holt they chirruped and wriggled in recognition. Circling them, she began to groom her own rudder and hind quarters while the cubs suckled vigorously.

For Lutra life settled into a routine of long hours spent curled round her cubs and brief fishing trips by night to satisfy her hunger. At the end of the month a rare heatwave hit the English countryside. Day after day the sun baked the land from a cloudless sky, crops shrivelled and wilted in the scorched fields, the tarred roads melted in the blinding noon heat.

The marsh fell silent; no birds sang; no breeze

stirred the reeds. Cattle huddled at watering places knee deep in the warm mud, flicking their tails against the buzz of flies. It was hot even in the otters' holt, so hot that Lutra had to go down to the water to drink in the daylight. The cubs lay panting, their pink mouths open and they would have died had not Lutra carried each in turn by the scruff of the neck to dunk it in the cooling water of the reed bed.

Although they developed slowly the cubs grew quickly in size and when a month old they weighed nearly 750 grams. Their eyes had begun to open, the slate-grey pupils showing through slits which daily grew wider. They could crawl now and were able to hold up their heads, peering at the light filtering through the entrance of the holt. They grew stronger, their eyes opened completely within a week and soon they crawled to the entrance of the holt when Lutra went fishing.

The cubs were seven weeks old when they first left the holt, and then it was only to relieve themselves a few steps from the entrance. By this time Lutra had stopped licking up their droppings.

While they were still small, Lutra ate what she caught on the nearest piece of dry land, but now she often returned carrying an eel into the holt and once a small flounder. At first the cubs took no notice of these strange objects, leaving their mother to eat in peace.

One night the male cub, larger and more adventurous than his sister, sniffed and then gingerly nibbled the tail of an eel while Lutra chewed its head. He was hungry and it tasted good. Within days both cubs had learned to eat anything Lutra brought home though they still suckled regularly as well.

The heatwave lasted over a month and when the first banks of rain cloud built up in the sky the cubs were two months old and weighed over one kilogram. They could run quite well by then and, though still too young to follow their mother on her nightly fishing trips, they came out of the holt as soon as it was dark to play rough and tumble games which soon flattened the nearby vegetation.

Everything new caught their attention. A grey feather from a wood pigeon's wing discovered by the female cub was a prized trophy until her brother seized it and ran off, only to drop it moments later. Often their games took the form of tag during which they raced round and round the old thorn tree until the ground was worn smooth. If one cub, straying, lost contact with the other, it uttered a high pitched whistle of distress which soon united them again. These were carefree days which were to end very shortly.

8
Man the Enemy

It was mid-September. The young mallard, hatched on the marsh, were strong on the wing. At dusk the family groups flew in formation to feed on the upland stubbles where corn, spilled from the combine harvesters, attracted them. Each year the stubbling time grew shorter as farmers used faster and heavier machinery to plough the land ready for the next crop. And each year many of the young ducks fell to the sportsman's gun on these nightly flights.

One day a small green van pulled off the road at the edge of the marsh and two men got out. From the back of the van they took a dozen traps made of stout wire, each ninety centimetres long with a treadle device in the centre and a spring-loaded hinged door at one end like a huge box mousetrap.

They were from the Ministry of Agriculture and were employed to control the coypu. Together they set off across the marsh, the turned down tops of their thigh-waders flapping around their knees. Keeping close to the embankment they headed towards the main dyke crossing the lesser drains on slippery planks.

Coypu make tracks in and out of the water rather like otters, but their habit of chewing the waterside vegetation together with their characteristic lozenge-shaped droppings easily distinguish them. Unlike otters they burrow freely in the banks and make no attempt to conceal their activities.

The tall reed called phragmites is a valuable crop on the marshes, being the best material for thatching buildings and is much in demand. Unfortunately the coypu, in addition to damaging the flood banks, like to eat young reeds.

On reaching the dyke the men took a bank each and began walking towards the thorn bushes. They found fewer signs of coypu than they had expected, but they set half a dozen traps in obvious runs. No attempt was made either to conceal or bait the traps, for the gentle slow-witted coypu trundling along his accustomed route takes no notice of a wire cage. If he comes up against the closed end he walks round it, if the open end – he walks into it and is caught.

The man on the bank nearest the road remembered the dry hummock with the thorn bushes and waded through the reeds towards it.

Pulling up his thigh-waders he pushed his way through the barrier of matted nettles, bramble and goose grass. It was hot work and he left the air heavy with the odour of sweat and stale tobacco. Passing close by the fallen thorn he stopped to examine the ground worn smooth by the otter cubs' games, and he noticed their spraint and the rounded tracks they left in the mud near the reeds. On the far side of the hummock, just clear of the water and hidden by rushes, he set a trap.

Back at the dyke he called across to his mate telling him about the otters. When they had set the last of their traps they turned inland down a track towards the road and so back to their van.

Inside the holt Lutra, curled round her cubs, had listened to the disturbance, and had smelled the man smell. At dusk she came out warily, stopping to sniff and listen. Ducks flew overhead, dark shapes on whispering pinions; unseen creatures rustled in the reed bed and a moorhen called in alarm, jerking its head back and forth and flirting the white feathers of its tail as it walked.

Satisfied that the men had gone, Lutra whistled to her cubs. They rushed out of the holt bumping into each other in their excitement. She led them straight to the water's edge, calling to them to follow as she swam into the reeds, but the cubs ran to and fro squeaking with fright, unable to bring themselves to leave the security of dry land. Once the male cub almost launched himself, paddling with his front paws but keeping his rear feet firmly on land, squeaking frantically for his mother. Lutra came back and without further ado seized him by the scruff, dragged him in and swam away carrying him with his head held just clear of the water. Once

in his mother's jaws the cub became silent and limp, his body offering least resistance, and when she dived he automatically closed his nostrils tightly and held his breath. At the far side of the reed bed she left the water and dropped the cub on the meadow, leaving him bedraggled and whistling forlornly as she disappeared to collect his sister whose squeals of distress she could still hear.

Soon both cubs were rolling and squirming in the grass, imitating their mother's actions. Their woolly coats lacked her waterproofing and they wore a crumpled look as they set off, following her across the marsh towards the main dyke like two bedraggled fur mittens. This was their first great adventure, but at nine weeks old they were too scared of being left behind to enjoy it. Instead they ran along like clockwork toys, bumping into each other, squeaking with alarm if Lutra drew too far ahead.

At the dyke she turned left, keeping to the short grass of the meadow where it was easier for the cubs to follow. Soon they came to a side ditch where the water lay deep and black, encrusted with a thick layer of duck-weed. Again Lutra transported the cubs one at a time and so they journeyed westward through the night.

Once the air suddenly became heavy with the acrid-sweet smell of cattle and steaming dung, stained green by grass grown lush from recent rains. They could hear the huge beasts exhaling like distant whales and could just make out their great shapes silhouetted against a sky paled by the light of the waning moon.

9
The Cubs' First Swim

They had covered more than three kilometres when Lutra stopped on the bank of the main dyke and led the cubs down through a jungle of tall thistles to a grassy shelf screened by sedges. She left them there, huddled together in tired silence, while she slipped into the water in search of food. She soon caught two small eels which she ate at the edge of the dyke, resting her hind feet on the muddy bank.

Sticklebacks swarmed in dense shoals and Lutra, diving through them, snapped up the silver-green fish, crunching on them as she swam at the surface. Her hunger dulled, she took the next eel back for her cubs. Pouncing on the writhing coils they seized an end each and played a boisterous tug-o-war until the female cub almost fell in the dyke and lost her grip on the eel's slippery tail. The male cub ran through the thistles on to the top of the bank pursued by his sister, but whenever she came near he danced away, the eel hanging limp from his jaws. When she finally gave up he settled down to chew it in peace.

Lutra was on the shelf eating another eel when the female cub returned, but when she came close her mother stopped and turned on her, chittering angrily, holding the cub down with one front paw across her back. Released, the cub sat watching her mother, not daring another attempt to filch a piece of the eel. Later on Lutra landed with another eel and only then did she allow the cub to feed.

After drying herself in the grass Lutra lay watching the water, her flat head resting on the ground, her hind legs stretched straight out behind her in that rubber-jointed attitude

peculiar to otters. Presently the cubs joined her, pushing their muzzles into her flank. The male cub stopped and playfully bit the fur of her neck. Finally Lutra turned on her side and suckled them.

An hour before dawn found the family nearly five kilometres from Thorn Bush holt and the disturbance caused by the coypu trappers. Lutra had no intention of returning there. Instead she led her cubs along the edge of a shallow ditch close to a reed bed until they came to the old wooden bridge. Once it linked two fields on the same farm, then some of the land had changed hands and the ditch became a boundary.

Both ends of the bridge had been sealed off with strands of barbed wire and brambles soon took over the no-man's land, their saw-toothed tendrils creeping out from either end to join and intertwine across the rotting timbers. More tendrils followed and within a few years the bridge became swamped beneath the green tide which hung in drapes over the ditch and billowed into one impenetrable thicket. Lutra remembered the darkness below the bridge and the dry black soil on which its timbers rested. It was a secret place, undisturbed by man.

She dug out a hollow between two cross

beams, right at the top of the bank underneath the planking. It was dry and dark and hidden. She curled herself round the cubs and slept.

The water in the ditch was shallow and clear. Apart from sticklebacks, it held little in the way of food and Lutra used it chiefly as a route to and from the main dyke on her nightly fishing trips. For the cubs it was a new playground and one which they explored with excited curiosity. The water fascinated them, and though neither had been brave enough to swim they paddled at the edge, sludged in the dark mud where the bank had been trodden down by cattle, and ducked their heads below the surface trying to catch mirrored stars in their mouths.

The male cub was the first to swim. He was ten weeks old and several times had almost let go of the bank with his hind feet. Then one

night the squeak and rustle of a vole on the far bank had been too much for his curiosity. Forgetting his fear he set off, dog-paddling uncertainly across the narrow ditch. He enjoyed the new sensation and was soon swimming with confidence. Diving was another matter; he found it easy to slip beneath the surface but much more difficult to stay down. Several times he bobbed up stern first, paddling in vain.

The female cub was nervous. Try as she would she could not force herself to leave the bank with her hind feet, though her body was afloat and her front feet paddled bravely. Then one night Lutra set off followed by her brother. Left alone the cub whistled piteously, running along the water's edge to keep abreast of them.

Every few paces she half succeeded in swimming, but always gave up. Then Lutra came back, pushed her muzzle against the youngster's face and lay still in the shallows. The cub climbed on to her rudder and Lutra shoved off. Suddenly the young otter was floating against her mother's flank. She tried desperately to climb on to her back, but Lutra slipped away, calling and the cub paddled after her.

As soon as they could swim, both cubs followed Lutra every evening when she went fishing. They swam one on each side of her rudder down the middle of the ditch. From their level the thistles atop each bank were silhouetted against the starry sky, tall as oaks.

Lutra still brought them fish, chiefly eels which they ate in the shallows or up on the grass after wild games of tag and tug-o-war. Every night they became more confident and more skilful in the water so that soon they played in the dyke rather than on land, wrestling and diving, spinning and porpoising, until the surface boiled silver in the starlight.

Fishing came naturally to them though they were over three months old before they caught more than a chance stickleback. They had no difficulty with small eels when they found them half buried in the mud, but for the most part they hunted for the fun of the chase and relied on Lutra when it came to a square meal. They still suckled regularly though at longer intervals.

Inland from the main dyke lay a lagoon fed by a brook which rose in the uplands ten kilometres away where springs of clear water welled up from fissures in the chalk deep underground.

With its shallows and soft mud, the lagoon was a favourite haunt of waders, redshank, snipe, godwits and dunlin. The otters often passed through it on their way to visit the stream leaving their tracks clearly visible in the glistening ooze.

The cubs enjoyed these journeys for, unlike the marsh dykes, the water in the stream was clear and sweet especially in the upper reaches

where it rippled over beds of gravel. One moonlit night the male cub dived to explore a patch of weed, and swimming along the bottom discovered a round pebble the size of a golf ball. Taking it between his front paws he rolled on to his back and tried to balance it on his chest. Each time it rolled off he caught it and continued to juggle until forced to the surface for air.

Diving again he found a larger stone which he dislodged by pushing his muzzle under one corner. As it turned over, a puff of sediment was carried by the current exposing a small lobster-like creature about seventy-five millimetres long. The cub seized it in his mouth only to be nipped by one of the pincer claws. Released, the crayfish flipped jerkily away propelled backwards by its flattened tail. The cub caught it again and crunched it between his teeth before continuing to play with it in his front paws. At the same time he rolled over and over just above the bed of the stream. Back at the surface he ate the crayfish and liked the sweet taste of its flesh.

Both cubs soon learned to dislodge stones in search of these delicacies and often they found small fish, gudgeon and loach which they chased and caught. The summer nights were carefree, and so long as the otters remained within the coastal marsh they were safe, for it was maintained as a nature reserve.

Gradually, imperceptibly the nights grew longer and colder, eels became fewer as the water temperature dropped and they buried themselves deep in the mud for their winter sleep. The skylarks stopped their song to the dawn and waterfowl patterned the sky in orderly flocks. The reed beds, golden-brown, bowed and sighed in the wind which sent the white thistledown blowing like snow across the marsh. Autumn was sliding away as winter took over. The otter cubs were growing up.

10
Winter

During the weeks that followed Lutra and her cubs remained in the marshes though they wandered far and were often absent for several days from the holt beneath the bridge. Once the dog otter joined them staying for two nights. He took little notice of the cubs, allowing them to nibble his fur and climb on his back and even occasionally to steal some of his catch.

As the days grew shorter the marsh began to acquire the bleak, austere atmosphere of winter. Thistles, turned brown, shivered in the wind; lapwings formed into flocks which flinked black and white like dominoes against the sky and ash-grey fieldfares, newly arrived from Norway, scattered across the short turf in search of insects.

At one end of the marsh a reed harvester clattered, scissoring the crisp stems, ejecting them in neatly tied bundles to be collected and carted away. No longer did men in thigh boots scythe the crop and tie it by hand.

The cubs, now five months old, were almost as big as Lutra. They caught much of their own food, but were still dependent upon her, even suckling from time to time, though her milk supply was beginning to diminish and of her four teats the front two were already dry.

December came in with a prolonged spell of rain which filled the reams and dykes. A spell of calm clear weather followed with a curiously amber tinge to the light. It was two days before full moon and the wind had backed into the north west. At dusk a bank of leaden cloud advanced inexorably across the sky.

In coast guard huts along the shore, and in the water authorities' pumping stations telephones rang – flood warning red!

Lutra needed no such warning; she was out with her cubs fishing in the main dyke when the first drops of rain fell. By then the wind was blowing strong, and in cramped wheelhouses men of the inshore trawler fleet wedged themselves and struggled to keep on course in a night grown black as pitch. Radios crackled the warning "North Sea gale force 8 rising to storm force 10 imminent."

By midnight the wind had increased to force 10 and it was behind the flood tide which, with all the force of the Atlantic to help it, was flowing south down England's east coast.

At first the wind had shrieked across the marsh, but now its anger rose to a deep roar as the storm drove the sea in inky blackness like two ancient gods of Greece combined to attack the land. Backed by the gale the North Sea built up into a solid wall of water which overwhelmed the coast defences.

The shingle ridge was breached in four places; farther along the coast the sand dunes went down like a pack of cards. In other places the seawall gave and the mountain of water swept inland devouring village and hamlet.

When dawn came the sea had retreated far out beyond the wide mudflats where flocks of Brent geese flew the tide edge, changing forma-

tion like billowing clouds of smoke. Along the coast men counted the drowned and salvaged their belongings. Lutra and her cubs were asleep, dry beneath a sueada bush on the highest point of the ridge, the only place the sea had left unconquered.

By noon the wind had eased and tattered clouds sped across the sky leaving patches of azure through which the sun shone briefly. Out beyond the shingle ridge the sea was returning, filling the creeks and gullies and flooding the saltings. Inland the great marsh lay inundated, a grey-brown lake where rafts of duck slept in peace after the night's buffeting.

As soon as the light began to fade Lutra led her cubs back to the estuary following the traditional route across the saltings and up the river to the seawall. They crossed the coast road in darkness, slipping down the bank on the landward side into the upper reaches of the estuary, now an inland sea where the great

reed beds stood in a metre of murky water.

The otters disliked the change. There was no dry land on which to rest, and fish were scattered and hard to find. Lutra headed upstream adjusting her pace for the benefit of the cubs. Only when the river narrowed between high banks to the north of the New Cut did she lead them out of the water to roll and dry themselves in the grass.

Usually there was a belt of reeds and glistening mud between the river and the foot of the embankment, but now the water had risen to within a metre of the top. They made one foray into the partially flooded grazing marsh where Lutra caught a moorhen. The cubs hungrily cleared up what little she left of the carcass.

When the eastern sky showed the first pale glimmer of the coming dawn, Lutra and her cubs were well inland, swimming up the flooded valley which averaged nearly one and a half kilometres across. The black shapes of trees, alders and willows and the stunted forms of blackthorn, broke up the silver expanse of water which spread to the foot of the higher land where the main road ran.

They came to a pollard willow standing knee deep in the flood. Once, long ago, it had been a great tree with branches sweeping upwards, but successive gales had torn them down leaving white scars which turned rotten with the years, hollowing out the main trunk. Lutra and her cubs scrabbled up inside and were soon fast asleep curled up together in the crown of the tree.

The following night they passed the pink farmhouse standing right at the edge of the flood and soon they came to the beck which flowed from the fen into the main river. In summer it was reduced to a mere trickle and the fen itself was dry enough in most places for a man to walk through it. Now the beck was swollen with flood water and the fen impassable except to otters and the wildfowl which wintered there.

Much of the area was reed bed, but in the drier places there were dense thickets of goat willow glowing bronze in the winter sunlight. The remains of old banks, where in a previous century men had dug peat for fuel, supported a few stunted oaks, their roots blanketed by emerald green moss soft as eiderdown.

Food was plentiful; there were fish, rudd and minnows in the beck, and tench in the nearby pools as well as moorhens and wild duck. Lutra knew from the sprainting places that the dog otter often came that way, and on their second night in the fen he came up from the river and joined in their hunting, leaving before dawn to lie up in a place of his own. They saw him regularly for over a week, then he disappeared to patrol the rest of his territory.

The cubs were nearly six months old and, though they stayed with Lutra, they caught their own food and the male was already as big as his mother. The female was smaller and less sure of herself. Quite often she tried to sneak up and snatch a fish which Lutra was eating only to be driven away with angry chitters. The two youngsters played together a great deal; games in which Lutra sometimes joined.

Other animals lived in the fen and often the otters saw a fox trotting along the edge of the reeds keeping to the dry ground in search of

pheasants which roosted in the willow scrub low enough to be stalked and seized. The foxes also caught moorhens and voles, burying their surplus prey by digging a shallow hole with their front paws, pushing the earth back with their noses, the whole action completed in a matter of seconds leaving no outward sign of their cache.

Lutra and the cubs remained in or near the fen for almost a month. The water subsided leaving the river valley fresh and green. Flotsam from the flood hung in clusters from the lower branches of willows and alders like crude birds' nests. Flocks of waders, lapwings and snipe and redshanks gathered to probe for food in the sodden turf. For the otters too, life was easier with the river flowing normally and fish for the catching. The weather was mild and on days of sudden sunshine men looked for signs of spring. But as so often happens the life of comparative plenty did not last for long.

11
The Freeze

The full moon of February rose like a huge opal gathering brilliance as the daylight faded. The nights were crisp and bright.

A cold wind blew fitfully driving flurries of snow, powdering the frozen ploughlands and bringing with it flocks of fieldfares and redwings, thrushes of the north, moving southwards in search of milder weather.

Soon it became clear that England was in for one of those rare cold spells born in Siberia. The shallow waters of the fen were the first to freeze, forcing Lutra and her cubs to return to the river.

As the temperature dropped, wildfowl poured into the valley, filling the night sky with the rustle of wings, the low chuckle of

mallard and the musical "whee-ohs" of drake wigeon come to feed on the short sweet grass. One night Lutra heard a strange bugling as fifteen great white birds swept low over the river; yellow-billed Bewick's swans, visitors from Russia, had joined the throng of migrants driven south by the intense frost.

Soon the meadows rang like iron under the horses' hooves. The dykes and ditches turned solid and redwings, always the first to suffer, sat about, their feathers puffed against the cold, becoming weaker by the hour through starvation. Many of them too feeble to fly died, and at night rats devoured the pathetic remains.

A strange stillness gripped the land, and at dawn Lutra watched the rooks straggling from their roost near the vicarage, a silent black rabble strung out over the valley in search of food. No time for the wheeling and cawing of spring, their flight was purposeful, almost desperate. Only the scavengers, crows and gulls and the killers – stoats, weasels and foxes – profited from the growing supply of frozen birds.

At first the river remained open, providing a safe retreat for the diving ducks, tufted and pochard, frozen out of lakes and gravel pits. Then ice pans began to form building up in the eddies and slack water, welding together until only the faster runs remained clear.

There was little cover left on the banks as the hemlock, hogweed and cowbane died, shrivelled and fell and with the increasing cold, Lutra as if forewarned, led her cubs downstream towards the brackish waters of the estuary.

They travelled by night diving in pursuit of fish, stopping to eat on the frosted bank and visiting the traditional sprainting places. Impervious to the cold the otters revelled in it, chasing one another out on to the meadow and back again, rushing headlong into the river in a shower of silver spray, making the reflected stars dance.

On a night of white cloud which hid the waning moon they heard a distant clamour, high-pitched and musical, the baying of sky-borne hounds. Presently they saw the dark forms of white-fronted geese, flying in V-shaped skeins, silhouetted against the pale sky. They too had arrived from the north in search of kinder weather. In the village men heard the geese and reckoned they foretold harder weather to come.

On the third night, the otters passed through the New Cut and out into the upper estuary. It was almost high water and the deep runnels which patterned the mud were already flooded. Fish were moving with the tide, flounders and sticklebacks which Lutra and the cubs caught without effort.

They reached the coast road an hour before midnight. Lutra was making for the distant saltmarshes where a small stream made its final bid to reach the sea through the muddied banks of a deep creek. Just inland lay a thicket of gorse and bramble where the soil was sandy and dry and where men rarely came.

Twice Lutra led her cubs up the bank to cross the road, and each time the noise of an approaching car caused her to turn back. There was more traffic than usual for the pubs had shut and men were going home. At the third attempt Lutra crossed the road, followed by the male cub, and ran down the bank on the opposite side. The female cub was about to follow when the headlights of a car rounding a bend sent her scurrying back.

When Lutra found the cub was not with her, she returned, calling in a high-pitched whistle. The cub answered from the far side of the road, started to cross then lost her nerve and ran back. Lutra called again, this time from farther away. The cub ran along the verge, frightened at being left behind. Lutra called again. Lights shone on all sides and the cub in blind panic rushed after her mother.

Two cars passed in opposite directions and in one the driver felt a bump. He sped on.

The cub had run straight into one of the car's rear wheels and such was the impact that her body was hurled back on to the grass verge. She lay there, silent and twitching; blood began to ooze from her nostrils and ears.

When the cars had gone Lutra called again. Hearing no answer she returned and found her cub. Gently she muzzled the body calling softly, and when it remained still she crossed the road again only to turn back, calling. She was joined by the male cub and for the next hour she crossed and re-crossed the road calling in vain.

Once she led the surviving cub nearly half a kilometre towards the saltings only to return in another attempt to recover the lost one. This time she nosed the lifeless body, dragging it a few paces by the scruff, but it was heavy and strangely cold.

Lutra remained nearby, returning again and again, calling for her lost cub, and only when daylight came and the early morning traffic began did she give up. That day she lay with the male cub under a bramble clump a few hundred metres away.

In the early afternoon two men in bright orange jackets walked one on each side of the road. They carried spades and were clearing grups in the verges which drained the surface water. One of them found the dead otter and picked it up. He knew where he could get a few pounds for its skin.

As soon as it was dark Lutra came back to the place and called for her cub. After a while she went away, followed by her son. When dawn came they curled up together in the security of the gorse thicket at the edge of the salting.

12
Spring

The cold weather lasted until the end of the first week in March, and during that time Lutra and her cub stayed in the coastal marshes and in the estuary, living on sticklebacks, flounders and small crabs.

Inland the dykes were frozen solid and the river remained free of ice only where it ran swiftly below the weirs and mill pools. Flocks of lapwings, their food supply locked in the hard ground, had resorted to the saltmarshes where they joined snipe and redshanks no longer able to probe in the muddy ditches and dykes of the meadows. Herons too moved down to the unfrozen waters of the estuary where they lined the banks at dawn. They looked just like grey sentries standing silent and still, watching for the movement of fish.

When the thaw came, the lambs' tails were hanging in yellow clusters from the hazel bushes and the silver-grey buds on the pussy willows were full and fluffy, soft as swan's down. Thrushes sang and lapwings tumbled and dived from the sky uttering their spring song, "peee-wee-weet ... peee-weet", dashing across the marsh in erratic flight as though out of control, their rounded wings making music from the air. Sometimes two or three males performed aerial acrobatics and song flights together.

Lutra heard them as she led the male cub back up the river. He was almost nine months old and although he followed her he was becoming much more independent; while at the same time her maternal bond was weakening and she no longer called when he wandered off. Sometimes he lay up for the day in a hiding place of his own.

They met the dog otter one April night not far from Thorn Bush holt. Eels were beginning to wake from their winter sleep buried in the mud and the otters were hunting them in the main dyke. Some of the eels were still torpid from their long hibernation and were easy to catch.

Several nights later all three otters moved

upstream heading for the old gravel workings below Decoy Wood. On the way they visited the mill pool where a big house stood overlooking the water, surrounded by well kept lawns and ancient trees. The owner, a keen naturalist and fisherman, had stocked the river with brown trout the biggest of which lived in the deep water of the pool.

The mill had been demolished years before, now the river swept through a sluice gate, before thundering down a concrete channel, dark with moss, to cascade into the pool from a culvert beneath the road. There the water foamed creamy-white like freshly poured beer, the myriad bubbles providing life-giving oxygen for the fish and plants.

The otters arrived in the pool shortly before midnight. From the river the house stood out against the black sky, its windows glowing orange from the lighted rooms within. Lutra and the dog otter soon caught a fat trout each. They ate them on the shingle spit where the stream divided at the tail of the pool. The cub had never seen trout before and was baffled by their speed. After several fruitless attempts he caught one in a bed of weed and carried it on to the lawn in front of the house.

The waterfall at the head of the pool attracted the otters and while the cub continued

to chase trout, Lutra and the dog otter played in the foaming torrent, diving and surfacing where the water boiled beneath the culvert, only to dive again into the vortex where the full weight of the river sucked them down, spinning them round and round and casting them up to the surface forty metres below. They enjoyed it and repeated the manoeuvre time and time again.

In the early hours they heard raised voices; light poured from the front door of the house and car engines revved loudly. The three otters watched from the centre of the mill pool, only their eyes and nostrils above the black surface of the water as the revellers went noisily home to bed.

Two hundred metres above the pool the river ran through a no-man's land of derelict cottages and a dark spinney hung with ivy. The place was dank, overgrown and seldom disturbed. Near the middle of the copse a wood pile had lain so long that most of the logs were rotten. Brambles and bindweed had smothered it so that little showed above the sea of nettles. The three otters crawled beneath the logs, hollowed out a space between the rotting timber and curled up together to sleep away the day.

With the arrival of spring, frogs and toads had gathered in their hundreds at the gravel pits to mate and lay their eggs. Already bubbles of frogs' spawn floated among the water plants along the edge of the pits in gelatinous masses like tapioca. A black spot in the centre of each egg would soon develop into a tadpole and those that were lucky enough to escape being eaten by predators, including larger tadpoles, would grow legs, lose their tails and after three months turn into tiny frogs.

The otters ignored the toads with their rough warty skins and their poison glands, but they played with the frogs, throwing the wretched creatures up in the air in a cat and mouse game before eating them.

Hordes of rats joined in the easy feast, stealing down to the water's edge in the darkness. They ate the frogs on the shore picking them clean of every morsel of flesh and leaving the skin turned neatly inside out.

One May evening Lutra was fishing above Heronry Wood. It was still daylight and a cuckoo called from far across the marsh; high above the river a snipe, looking no bigger than a starling, flew up and down over its territory diving repeatedly, its tail spread, so that the air rushing through the stiff outer feathers made a thrumming noise that carried far.

The dog otter had stayed behind in the gravel pits and Lutra had not seen her cub for several days, so that when an otter swam towards her she assumed he had returned. But the other otter was a yearling female which had been born and brought up on another river and was searching for a territory of her own. Lutra swam after her in silence. Only when she caught up did she chitter with rage and rush at the interloper with harsh screams chivvying her down the river and out of her territory. In two years' time the young female would mate with Lutra's son. But in the interval both would spend their time, wandering, ranging far along the coast and into other estuaries before they would be able to lay claim to their own stretch of river.

The summer was well advanced when Lutra came again into breeding condition. A few days earlier the dog otter had driven her son downstream and had followed Lutra to Decoy Wood where they lay up in the hollow alder.

In time they mated, wandering together for several days before the dog moved on leaving Lutra on her own.

During the weeks that followed she made several visits to a dyke that joined the river a kilometre above Heronry Wood. It was deep and reed-fringed, and its course across the marsh was marked by the old willows growing on its banks and by the line of overgrown spoil from dredging done long ago. Beneath one of the trees Lutra dug a holt deep into the dry earth, and as the time approached she lined it with twigs, reed heads and with the dank tresses of water crowfoot.

Early one September morning she gave birth to three cubs, and once again she knew the all-consuming ties of motherhood. The cubs were only a few days old when the dog otter visited them. As his head appeared in the burrow leading to the holt Lutra huffed at him and the cubs, disturbed by her movement, began to twitter. The dog otter drew back and went on his way.

Two nights later he visited the fen, returning down the beck to the main river as day broke. He swam upstream towards Heronry Wood and leaving the river made a temporary couch beneath some brambles at the edge of the osier carr and was soon fast asleep. An hour later the keeper passed that way and his spaniel chased a rabbit into the thicket. The dog otter woke with a start and made a dash for the river. At the sound of the shot he felt a numbing pain. Panic stricken he struggled towards the water, but his spine was shattered and his hind legs dragged uselessly. The keeper ran forward and at the second shot the dog otter rolled over, pawing the air with his front feet while the blood trickled from his mouth.

Lutra heard the distant shots and raised her head before curling more tightly around her cubs.

Word list

BECK a small brook or stream

DYKE a man-made ditch, water-course or drainage channel

FEN a low area of marsh or bog

GRUP a small drainage channel dug in roadside verges to remove surface water from the road

HOLT an otter's burrow or den, often in a river bank beneath tree roots; or it may be a natural cave among rocks or boulders away from the water's edge

HUMMOCK hillock, knoll or higher ground, especially in a marsh

NUTRIA the fur of the coypu, an aquatic rodent introduced to Britain and Europe from South America

OSIER CARR an area of willow trees growing at the edges of a fen or swamp

RUDDER an otter's tail

SPINNEY a small wood or thicket

SPRAINT an otter's faeces or droppings